20th Century Tool Shed

poems by

Robert Dreesen

Finishing Line Press
Georgetown, Kentucky

20th Century Tool Shed

Copyright © 2020 by Robert Dreesen
ISBN 978-1-64662-188-0 First Edition
All rights reserved under International and Pan-American Copyright Conventions. No part of this book may be reproduced in any manner whatsoever without written permission from the publisher, except in the case of brief quotations embodied in critical articles and reviews.

ACKNOWLEDGMENTS

I want to thank Martin Ogolter for the cover design and Warren van Tassel for the author photo.

Publisher: Leah Maines

Editor: Christen Kincaid

Cover Art and Design: Martin Ogolter

Author Photo: Warren van Tassel

Printed in the USA on acid-free paper.
Order online: www.finishinglinepress.com

Author inquiries and mail orders:
Finishing Line Press
P. O. Box 1626
Georgetown, Kentucky 40324
U. S. A.

Table of Contents

The Tool Shed 1

i. The Shovel 2

ii. The Hammer 3

iii. The Pliers 4

iv. The Machete 5

v. The Screwdriver 6

vi. The Axe 7

vii. The Crow Bar 8

viii. The Skilsaw 9

ix. Nails and Screws 10

x. Nuts and Bolts 11

xi. The Vice 12

xii. The Ratchet 13

Makers in America: the 21st Century 14

*In a small nation
With few folk,
Tools abound,
But are not put to use.*

—Lao-Tzu (tr. John Minford)

The Tool Shed

Just in front of the oak woodland sloping to the chalk bluffs,
Buffalo grass holds its own.
All around, Canada thistle, birds-foot trefoil,
Dog wood, buckthorn, and St. John's wort—
Aggressive species—invade and expand,
And have been since the beginning of the last century.

Fire every decade—total war—
Would have saved a lot of pulling, cutting,
Hoeing, spraying, and blasting.
Instead of rose bushes and silver buffaloberry
Surrounding the shed,
Gray-headed coneflowers, cockleburs,
Cedar trees, hemp, and poison ivy
Shroud canisters, rope, and wire,
Pitch forks, hoes, corn shovels, flat blades,
And the off-hand implements to ease human problems.

For decades the rusted latch has rattled;
The door flinches and pulls back.
Smells of oil, metal, and wood;
Dirty oil, dirty metal, dirty wood,
Oily and dirty benches, scarred benches.
On the rough-sawn splintered walls
Rusted nails carry prodigal tools
Waiting to be useful,
Handy as a man with skills,
With leather gloves, but no wristwatch.
Everything's in its place and everything's
Been used before, knows its role.

Outside, locusts roar and swallows feed in parabolas.
Vultures circle so close to the ground
You can see their skull caps.
Here nothing lasts long, but the tools and the shed.
Lorca knew this as he walked to his grave.

i.   The Shovel
for Pat Noecker

is
willful,
God of the Old Testament
before He "got religion."
Cutting roots
as well as
worms,
complicit in tyranny,
it can't be had
like a hammer,
and only when
you put your foot down
will it listen;
even then
it's too late;
for it's someone else's foot
on top of you.

ii. The Hammer

Immortalized by song,
the hammer is the oldest tool
in the shed
and confident,
even though it can fly off the handle.
Rim rod straight
with nerves
of steel,
it delivers blow after blow,
rings when striking true,
clamors when lied to.
Clean and balanced,
solid,
its profile is noble
as a dictator with a pig's snout.
Hands never lie
and this killer has claws.
Its only shame…
its stammer.

iii.   The Pliers

This player is
the utility infielder
of the shed
and a fascist's dream:
"is it safe," he asks
in his sleep,
and not to sheep.
It is safe
to assume
this fingernail puller
is no fool and will make it big
to pull what at its root
is less at home
in heaven than in hell;
and might be why
it's held together
by a nut;
plying its trade
from hip to hip in holster
for anyone who wants to be
known as a man
who gets things done.
The six-shooter of tools
is cool practicality.

iv.   The Machete

Aka corn knife,
aka poor man's battle axe,
aka broad-bladed bloodying knife—
is for culling or killing.
It is
the weapon of choice
for rural insurrectionists,
revolutionaries and slaves.
No other tool in the shed
dulls the senses
as this plastic-handled
loose-riveted
palm pincher,
enemy of Hutus and Tutsis,
farm boys and authorities.
Even God winces
when hearing its chops.
Rusty and dullest of tools,
of cutters in history,
with as many nicks as kills,
if this menace doesn't cut you
it will hate you.

v.   The Screwdriver

Innocuous handyman,
you're not to be trusted.
You find the grooves
and all too often
strip
them blind;
and then it's all palm,
push and turn, push
and turn until
nothing
remains.
A penchant for eyes,
you serve in a kill
for the knife.
You're a grind
and know the drill
will have its day,
but there is no shed
that does not see you.
Eventually you are
found out
and thrown away—
rusted as history—
the torturer's
afterthought.

vi. The Axe

Awkward,
unbalanced,
uncertain and
always getting
stuck,
this one—
though its status in the shed is
questionable
among the well-bred—
has a golden pedigree.
Despite its low IQ,
it counts—it can,
better than any other tool—
presidents and folk heroes
as benefactors.
A fireman's first,
it will forever be
contemporary.
Still, it's
the "crooked
timber of humanity."

vii. The Crow Bar

Where is that Jimmy
when I need him,
the prohibitionist asked.
He might have meant
the wrecking bar.
This big daddy with the swan's neck
has the most leverage
in the shed
and gets things done;
a rare sighting, like
the white rhino
or snow leopard,
it has a forked tongue
and is well hung.
The tyrant's spoon in bed,
this double-dealing ripper
wrecks homes and lives in broad day light.
You can hear its work, its
ripping and tearing.
It does not fly straight.

viii. The Skilsaw

This oxymoron
is a sadist
and the loudest tool
in the shed.
It always screams
and loves to cut
arms and legs.
Badly brought up,
egotistical, petulant, vane,
sitting on the bench
with its coat of arms
and shining armor,
it kicks like a mule
when it doesn't get its way
and often bites
the hand that feeds it.
And yet we continually go to it,
thinking it will toe the line
for us,
follow the straight and narrow,
that it will
stay true, as it boasts;
demonstrating that the tool we choose,
just as the fool that rules,
says more about us
than about that tool.

ix.   Nails and Screws

will either put it to us or
pin us down.
Pitch, twist,
pound and wrench,
explode, penetrate, and maim,
affix to death,
they're Christianity's staple
and anarchy's pluralistic mini-missiles—
always on
the wrong side
of history.
Instruments of torture,
they are the strongest verbs
and most destructive nouns
in the shed;
to be kept out of reach
of children
if not the dead.

x.   Nuts and Bolts

of life,
you're all metaphor
and play fast and loose
with history.
A mouthful—
the glove of gangsters
and fascists,
David's preferred weapon
had he the steel—
you're forever coming undone
when not blown up
on a bridge
or blown down
with a crane.
Your only attribute?
You cannot be matched
in your particularity, your
singularity;
stripped of universality,
there's only
one
for you.

xi.   The Vice

is stronger than Stalin's mustache,
its grip tighter than Hitler's formations.
When not mounted properly,
this muscle head will
drop everything
and fuck you.

xii.　The Ratchet

This six-toed raccoon
can't be fooled
into complicity
by mere nuts and bolts,
despite its felicity.
Its dance—
one step forward,
four steps backward,
click click click click—
is uniquely American
and anti-fascist.
Versatile and
efficient,
it's a renaissance tool—
of no use to fools
and strongmen.
A hymn to freedom…
Ratchet it up, baby.

Makers in America: The 21st Century

When from the battle sky, lies
Fall like heavy snow,
Obscuring in the Linden tree and Maplewood,
The male and female cardinal,
Cracking limbs with plastic whips
And breaking branches,
We'll put on our boots and coats, our gloves,
And shovel the truth like Dr. Zhivago.
We'll spread salt and gravel on the road
Of history, and the chorus will sing:
"How hard this life and long our way of stone."

Reckoning worth with blisters and sweat,
Faces unseen, our backs and hands, they
Never lie,
Butchers, cobblers, farriers and tailors—
Aristocrats of craft, the only aristocracy left—
Will go door to door plying their trade,
Doing the bidding of their
"One-man revolution,
The only revolution that's coming."

When half-truths and counter-facts
Come out of the sodden ground at night,
So many fat worms making holes in the firmament—
Boom, boom, boom—
Leaving silos of dirt as evidence of veracity,
We'll grab our flash lights and gallon tins
And firmly pull them out, slowly,
Vigilant about their viscous elasticity.

Milliners, knife sharpeners, tinkerers—poets!—
Will make a mulch from the tabloid news,
Kneading and mixing lies for worm food,
Careful not to breathe the dust of daily lives.
From bait shops and pickup trucks
A dozen lies per pint will be sold
Until some Fisher King casts his filament of truth
Thru "the piercing light of reality"
And catches the bloated leviathan below.

www.ingramcontent.com/pod-product-compliance
Lightning Source LLC
LaVergne TN
LVHW041526070426
835507LV00013B/1853